SABRINA FISHER REECE

Why Are You So Mean?

The Hidden Truth About Pain, Projection and Human Behavior

First published by In59Seconds Publishing 2026

First edition

ISBN: 978-1-971622-77-4

This book was professionally typeset on Reedsy.
Find out more at reedsy.com

To every soul who has ever been called mean, difficult, or too much. You were created from love, and love is still who you are.

Contents

Introduction

There is a version of you that the world may have come to recognize before they ever took the time to truly understand you. A version that reacts quickly, speaks directly, carries a certain edge, or holds a presence that makes people pause before they say certain things around you. You may have heard it before, maybe in subtle ways or maybe said plainly, that you are mean, that you have an attitude, that you are difficult, that you are a little too much, or that people have to handle you a certain way. Over time, those labels can begin to settle in, shaping how others see you and, eventually, how you begin to see yourself. What often goes unseen is the truth or root cause beneath that surface.

This book is for anyone who has ever been misunderstood in that way, for anyone who has ever been labeled as distant, mean, or hard to deal with, while quietly knowing that there is something more within them. It is for the person who feels the tension between how they show up in the world and who they truly are inside, for the one who knows there is kindness within them, love within them, and a softness that has not always had the chance to be expressed to others. It is for the person who never set out to become guarded, reactive, constantly offended or emotionally distant, but somehow found themselves there over and over again. Their identity has been shaped by experiences they did not fully understand and emotions they were never taught how to process.

There comes a point where the way you have been seen by others starts to feel easier to accept than trying to explain who you really are. The labels stick, the reactions are always the same, and eventually it can feel like there is no reason to fight against it anymore. So you lean into it and accept the label, you go along with it. It becomes your identity and you allow the world to believe that this is just who you are, even when something deeper inside of you knows that is not the full truth. Beneath that exterior, there is still a desire to connect with others, to feel understood, to give love freely and to receive it without fear or hesitation. We were all made in the image of God and God is pure love. So are you.

Even if it has felt buried for a long time, even if you have carried that version of yourself longer than you ever intended, that wonderful part of you has never left. It has been waiting, quietly, beneath the surface, for the moment where you are ready to acknowledge it again and allow it to come forward.

No one is born hateful and combative. No one is inherently mean or angry, no matter what genetic traits you may think you inherited from your parents or what you have been told about yourself over time. At your core, you were not created to be harsh, reactive, or closed off. There was always something pure, something open, something loving within you from the very beginning, and it is still there.

Somewhere along the journey of your life, something happened. For some, it was loss. For others, it was abuse, abandonment, betrayal, trauma, disappointment, or moments that were simply too overwhelming to fully process at the time. Life has a way of placing experiences in front of you that shape how you learn to respond, and when those experiences are painful, confusing, or left unresolved, they do not just fade away on their own. They settle quietly into your thoughts, into your emotions, and into your reactions to certain situations. The begin influencing how you move through the world in ways you may not even be fully aware of. Most importantly, they play a significant role in shaping your self esteem. When you do not feel good about who you are, when you question your value or your worth, it becomes difficult to show love to others in a healthy way when you have not yet learned how to extend that same love to yourself.

I want you to know that I understand this, not from a distant place, but from personal experience. I have lived through a tremendous amount of hurt. I have experienced trauma that shaped how I saw the world and how I saw myself within it. There were seasons in my life where I distanced myself from people, not because I did not care, but because I was afraid to care too deeply. I had already experienced what it felt like to lose, and somewhere inside of me, I made the decision that it was safer to keep people at a distance than to risk feeling that kind of pain again. At the time, I did not see it as fear. I saw it as strength. I saw it as control. Looking back now, I understand it for what it truly was, which was protection.

When you have been through traumas that the human heart was never meant to carry alone, and no one teaches you how to process those experiences in a healthy and supportive way, you naturally find another way to cope. You learn how to protect yourself the best way you know how, even if you do not realize that is what you are doing in the moment. That protection is not a flaw. It is not something to be ashamed of. It is a normal response. It is something that developed because, at one point in your life, you needed it.

That protection can take many forms. It can look like distance, where you keep people at arm's length so they cannot get close enough to hurt you. It can sound like sharp, harsh words that come out quickly, before anyone has the chance to say something that might affect you. It can feel like confrontation, defensiveness, control, or a constant sense of readiness, as if you have to stay one step ahead of everything and everyone just to feel safe. Over time, that protection becomes a huge wall, and that wall can easily be misunderstood.

What you built to keep yourself safe can be seen by others as being mean, insensitive, or unapproachable. People may only see the reactions, the tone, or the distance, without ever understanding what it took for you to build those layers in the first place. What they see is the surface. What they do not see is the pain, the confusion, the loss, or the experiences that shaped you into someone who felt like they had to protect themselves in that way, and that matters.

When you begin to understand that your behavior did not come from nowhere, something inside of you begins to soften. Not in a way that makes you weak, but in a way that allows you to see yourself with more compassion, more patience, and more truth.

This book is not here to judge that part of you. It is here to understand it. It is here to gently walk you through the truth that who you are is not the same as how you have learned to protect yourself. It is here to help you see that beneath the reactions, beneath the labels, and beneath the patterns that may have followed you for years, there is still something wonderful and whole, something loving, and something deeply worthy that has always been there. As you begin to see yourself in that light, something else begins to shift as well. The way you see other people begins to change.

The next time you encounter someone who feels difficult, someone who seems cold, dismissive, or even unkind, there is an opportunity to pause before reacting. Instead of immediately deciding who they are based on that moment, consider the possibility that there is more beneath the surface. Consider the possibility that they, too, have experienced something that shaped how they show up. Consider the possibility that what you are seeing is not their truth, but their protection.

That does not mean you allow behavior that disrespects you or crosses your boundaries. It means you begin to see people with a deeper level of awareness, one that allows space for compassion without losing yourself in the process.

Because the truth is, every person you encounter is carrying something.

Every person is navigating their own experiences, their own pain, and their own journey in ways that are not always visible. God did not create anyone to be mean, cold, or disconnected. At the core, every person was created from a place of love. What life does, through circumstances and experiences, is shape how that love is expressed or, in some cases, hidden.

This book is an invitation, to understand yourself in a deeper way. on a deeper more intimate level. It's an invitation to release the belief that who you have been is who you must continue to be, and approach both yourself and others with more compassion, more awareness, and more truth.

Because when you begin to understand the "why" behind the behavior, everything starts to make sense, and when things begin to make sense, something inside of you becomes ready to change for the better.

1

It Was Never Really About You

For a long time, I told myself that I was just a strong person with a sharp edge, someone who did not tolerate disrespect and refused to let anyone get over on me. That explanation felt easier to hold onto than the truth, because the truth required me to look at something deeper that I was not ready to face. Beneath that surface, anger was always there, steady and waiting, rising quickly at the smallest shift in tone, the slightest feeling of being dismissed, the faintest hint that I was not being valued the way I believed I deserved. I reacted fast, spoke sharply, and protected myself before anyone had the chance to fully hurt me, believing at the time that this constant readiness made me strong, when in reality it was a sign that something inside of me had never been given the space to heal.

It took me years to understand that anger is rarely just about the moment in front of you. Most people talk about anger as if it is simply attitude or temperament, as if it exists on its own without context, but they do not talk about the grief that sits underneath it, the hurt, disappointment or abandonment that quietly shapes how you see yourself, or the trauma that was never processed because you were too young to even understand what was happening while it was happening.

Anger became my armor long before I ever realized I was protecting anything, and by the time I began to question it, that armor had become so familiar that it felt like part of who I was.

My story did not begin in a place of safety or stability. My biological mother struggled with drug addiction, and when I was only a few months old, during one of her binges, she placed me inside a suitcase, closed it, and attempted to take my life because she said I cried too much as a baby. By the grace of God, I survived, not because of anything I did, but because it simply was not my time, and because someone stepped in who changed the entire course of my life.

That person was my grandmother, a strong, loving woman from Dallas, Texas, who made a decision that would shape everything that followed. She did not hesitate. She took me and my sister into her home and into her heart, providing a level of stability, structure, and unconditional love that my mother was not able to give at that time. I was only three months old, and my sister was eleven months old, and at sixty-nine years old, my grandmother chose to dedicate her senior years to raising us. She had already raised her own children, and her youngest son, Jesse Paul Fisher, was our father, which made us her only granddaughters through him, yet she stepped into that role again without question.

She was an amazing woman in every sense of the word. She taught us about God in a way that felt real and grounded, not forced or distant, but present in everyday life. She showed us how to cook, how to care for a home, how to carry ourselves, and how to treat people with respect. More than anything, she gave us consistency and a solid foundation in life. She gave us a sense of belonging. She created an environment where we felt safe, where we felt seen, and where we felt loved in a way that was steady and reliable. In a world that had already introduced me to instability before I could even speak, she became everything a parent is supposed to be.

For most of my childhood and even into adulthood, I did not walk around thinking about that early experience in a conscious way. It was something I knew, something I could share when telling my story, but it was not something I allowed myself to truly feel or fully understand. It remained in the background, quietly influencing more than I realized, shaping how I responded to the world without ever being fully acknowledged. I never stopped to consider what it means for a child to grow up knowing that the person who gave them life could not care for them, or how that beginning might affect the way I learned to trust, to connect, or to feel safe in relationships. Those deeper questions stayed buried for a long time, and in their place, reactions began to form.

The woman who became my foundation, my sense of stability, and the one person who made me feel safe in a way I could rely on was my grandmother. She raised me with discipline, with values, and with a consistent presence that made me feel like I belonged somewhere, like I mattered in a way that was steady and real. She corrected me when I was wrong, supported me when I struggled, and loved me in a way that filled the spaces that had once been empty. She was not just my caregiver, she was my world, and for a long time, she was the reason I felt grounded and loved at all.

Then, in a single moment, everything changed in a way that no one could have ever prepared me for. At seventeen years old, I witnessed my grandfather, the man my grandmother had been married to for over three decades, take her life in front of me with a single gunshot wound to the head. That was the day my entire life changed. It did not just take her away from me, it shattered something deep inside of me that I did not yet have the language or understanding to describe. In an instant, the sense of safety I had finally come to know disappeared, replaced by shock, confusion, and a kind of overwhelming pain that does not settle easily into words. It felt as if every bit of hope I had in humanity drained out of me in that moment.

Some experiences divide your life into before and after, and that was mine. Everything I thought I could depend on, everything that made me feel grounded and secure, was taken in a violent and tragic way that was completely out of my control. My life would never be the same after that day. We had already lost our father when we were just ten and eleven years old, our mother was still out in the world struggling with addiction, and now the one person who gave us stability, unconditional love, and a safe, warm home was gone. At seventeen, I was left carrying wounds so deep that I could not even begin to understand them, let alone process them.

Life did not pause to allow me to grieve or make sense of what had just happened. Thirty days later, I was expected to put on a cap and gown, walk across the stage at Centennial High School in Compton, California, and step into adulthood as if something inside of me had not just been completely broken. There was no time, no space, and no guidance for processing that kind of loss. Therapy was not something people talked about the way they do now, and there were no tools handed to me that could help me understand how to carry that level of grief while still functioning. I did what I thought I had to do. I kept moving. I kept going. I pushed everything down as far as I could so it would not interfere with what was expected of me.

Stepping into adulthood already felt uncertain to me, but doing it without the emotional support system most people rely on made it even more difficult to navigate. Losing my father at such a young age had already created a void that I did not know how to fill, and with my mother still out in the world battling addiction, there was no safety net to fall back on, no place where I could fully land emotionally and feel supported in the way a young person needs. By the time I was nineteen, I entered into marriage, stepping into a role that required emotional stability, communication, and understanding that I had never been taught. I carried unprocessed grief, confusion, and trauma into a life that required connection, without fully understanding what I was bringing with me or how deeply it would affect the way I showed up.

At that time, none of it had a name in my mind. I did not call it trauma. I did not recognize the signs of what I now understand to be post-traumatic stress. What I believed instead was much simpler, and much more misleading. I told myself that I had a bad temper, that I was strong, that I was just a little sassy, someone who spoke their mind, someone who did not let people get over on them. In my mind, that version of me felt powerful. It felt like control. It felt like protection. What I could not see then was that it was actually a response, a carefully built wall designed to keep people at a distance so I would never have to experience the kind of loss and heartbreak that had already shaped my life.

Looking back now with a level of awareness I did not have then, I can clearly see that my anger was not random, and it was not something I was born with. It was rooted in two defining experiences that changed the way I saw the world and myself within it. Being abandoned by my mother at the very beginning of my life planted a seed of rejection and instability that I did not have the capacity to understand as a child. Witnessing the violent murder of my grandmother, the one person who gave me consistent love, safety, and guidance, shattered any sense of security I had managed to build. Those two moments, one at the very beginning of my life and one at seventeen, created wounds that ran deep, shaping how I responded to everything that came after that.

Underneath the anger that people saw in my twenties and thirties was a mixture of grief that had never been processed, fear that had never been soothed, and a deep sense of abandonment that had never been healed. The version of me that people labeled as mean or having an attitude was not who I was at my core. It was who I became in response to pain I did not understand. That sharpness, that quick reaction, that willingness to tell someone off before they could hurt me, all of it was rooted in a need to feel in control, to protect myself, and to avoid ever feeling that level of loss again.

From the outside, my life began to take shape in ways that looked productive and put together. I worked hard, built businesses, I bought a home and kept moving forward in ways that suggested I had everything under control. Internally, there was always a quiet tension, a sense that something could go wrong at any moment, a constant awareness that stability could be taken away just as quickly as it had been before. When situations did not go the way I expected, when people disappointed me, or when something felt even slightly off, my reactions were never just about what was happening in that moment. They were amplified by all the fear and pain I had carried for years, everything I had buried, and everything I had never taken the time to understand.

That version of me did not appear overnight. It developed gradually through repeated patterns of reacting instead of understanding, protecting instead of processing, and defending instead of healing. Each time I justified my behavior, it reinforced the belief that it was necessary, that it was part of who I was, and that without it, I would be exposed in a way that felt unsafe. Over time, it became familiar. It became my identity.

It was not until my reactions began to cost me something meaningful that I was forced to pause and ask myself a question I had avoided for years. Why am I this angry? That question did not bring immediate clarity, and it was not easy to sit with, but it opened a door that I could no longer ignore. It required me to go back and look at the parts of my life I had spent years pushing aside, to connect experiences I had never fully processed, and to begin understanding how they had shaped me.

I was not just angry at people or situations. I was angry at my life. I was angry at God for allowing certain terrible things to happen in my life. I was angry at the world for feeling unfair and unpredictable. I was pissed off at my mother for choosing drugs over her own children. I was carrying anger that had been building for years, and it was not going to disappear on its own. It needed to be acknowledged, understood, and worked through in a way that allowed something different to take its place in my life.

If you see yourself anywhere in this, I want you to understand something clearly. Anger is not always who you are. Quite often it is a reaction to deep seeded pain. Sometimes it is a reflection of what you have been through, a response that developed when you did not have the tools, the support, the understanding or the emotional intelligence to process something in a healthier way. We have all been there. But that does not make it harmless, and it does not excuse behavior that hurts others, but it does mean there is something underneath it that deserves your attention.

This book is not here to judge that part of you. It is here to help you understand it, to explore where it comes from, and to begin separating what happened to you from who you are. Because once you start to see that clearly, something begins to shift in a way that changes the direction of your life.

The anger starts to make sense, and once it makes sense, it becomes something you can finally begin to release.

2

The Moment I Realized It Was Me

There was a time in my life when I truly believed my temper was simply part of who I was. I did not hide it or question it in any meaningful way, and in many moments, I even justified it as a strength. I told myself that I was passionate, that I stood up for myself, and that I refused to tolerate disrespect from anyone. Raising my voice, reacting quickly, and making sure people understood exactly how I felt became normal behavior, something I leaned into instead of examining. Looking back now with a deeper level of awareness, I can see that what I was calling strength was actually something much more fragile and much more unresolved.

Running a business only intensified everything that was already inside of me. As a salon owner, I convinced myself that maintaining control meant being strict, dominant, and at times emotionally explosive. I had created detailed systems, clear expectations, and structured rules for my staff, and when those standards were not met, I felt justified in responding strongly. It became easy to believe that my reactions were necessary, that without that level of intensity things would fall apart or my staff would run over me. I even joked about it, brushing it off as part of my personality, blaming it on being a Leo or anything else that made it sound light, anything that would allow me to avoid looking at what was really happening beneath the surface. The truth is, I did not know there was anything deeper to look at.

At that time in my life, I was moving through the world at five foot two, carrying the weight of loss, trauma, and confusion that I had never fully processed. I had already experienced abandonment, I had witnessed unimaginable tragedy, and I was coming out of a marriage that reflected the state I was in internally more than I understood at the time. I found myself in a relationship with a man who hit women, and while I want to be very clear that I am not angry with him as I speak about this now, I also recognize that I accepted behavior that should never have been accepted. That acceptance did not come from strength. It came from unhealed wounds and the fear of not being loved..

When you have experienced trauma, especially at a young age, your understanding of love, safety, and connection can become distorted in ways that are difficult to recognize while you are living in it. After everything I had been through, I did not have a clear example of what healthy love looked like. I did not fully understand what it meant to be treated with care, respect, and emotional safety. In many ways, I was still trying to make sense of relationships through the lens of pain I had never healed.

Looking back now, I can see that the hardened version of myself that I developed during that time was not who I truly was. It was who I believed I needed to be in order to survive. I built that version of myself to protect against being hurt again, to make sure no one could break me in the way I had already been broken. I thought that being tough, being guarded, and staying in control would keep me safe. I was wrong.

What I did not understand then is that true strength is not found in how hard you become, but in how willing you are to heal what made you feel like you had to become that way in the first place.

Over time, something began to shift in a way that I could not ignore.

I started to notice the difference between people who respected me and people who feared me. On the surface, both groups followed the rules, both showed up, and both did what was expected, but the energy behind it was completely different. Fear creates compliance, but it does not create connection, loyalty, or trust. Respect, on the other hand, grows from consistency, fairness, and emotional stability. The more I paid attention, the more I realized that my behavior was not building the kind of environment I thought it was. Instead of strengthening my leadership, it was creating distance, and underneath all of it, there was a truth I had not fully acknowledged, which was that I was afraid to let people get too close because I had never truly healed from what I had been through.

The moment that forced me to confront this in a real and undeniable way came during a staff meeting that I will never forget. I had nine employees at the time, and the weight of running a business was heavy on me. Every mistake, every complaint, every issue that arose fell back on me, and the pressure had been building for a long time. I was addressing general concerns, trying to communicate expectations without singling anyone out, but one employee kept interrupting me, asking repeatedly if I was talking about her. Her tone was sharp, defensive, and challenging, and something inside of me reacted instantly, not just to her words, but to something much older that had nothing to do with that moment.

People often describe anger as seeing red, and in that moment, I understood exactly what that meant. My vision shifted, my body reacted, and everything around me faded except for her. I reached for an object on my desk and for a split second, I lost control of myself in a way that scared me. Something inside of me stopped me just as quickly as the reaction rose, and I sat back down, took a breath, and made the decision to let her go, but I did it calmly. That moment stayed with me long after the meeting ended because I knew how close I had come to making a decision that could have changed everything in my life.

What shook me was not just the situation itself, but the realization of how much I had to lose. I had built a business, established a reputation, created stability for myself, and in one impulsive moment, all of it could have been taken away. That kind of awareness forces you to see yourself honestly, without excuses, without justification, and without hiding behind the stories you have been telling yourself. I could no longer pretend that my anger was harmless or that it was simply part of my personality. It had reached a point where it was dangerous, not just for others, but for me as well.

Instead of continuing down the same path, I made a decision that required humility in a way I had not experienced before. I chose to seek help. Being angry and snappy all the time is not cute or healthy. I found a anger management class. Walking into anger management was not something I was forced to do, and it was not something anyone told me I had to do. It was a decision I made because I could no longer ignore what I had seen in myself. Sitting in a space where most people were there because they had been ordered to be by the court system forced me to confront my own reality even more clearly. I was there because I chose to be, and that choice marked the beginning of a different direction in my life.

Working with someone who understood emotional behavior on a deeper level opened my eyes to something I had never fully considered before. Anger is rarely the first emotion. It is often what rises to the surface because it feels stronger, more protective, and more controlled than what is underneath it. Beneath my anger lived years of grief, fear, disappointment, un-diagnosed PTSD, and unresolved pain that I had never taken the time to process. What I had been reacting to in the present was often connected to something from my past, something that had been triggered without me even realizing it.

Understanding triggers changed everything for me. A trigger is not just what happens in front of you. It is the meaning your mind and body attach to that moment based on everything you have experienced before. For years, I believed my reactions were about what people were doing in the moment, their tone, their behavior, their actions, but what I began to see was that those situations were only activating something that was already there. Feelings of disrespect, abandonment, and being dismissed were not new experiences for me. They were familiar, and when they were triggered, my response was not just about the present moment. It was layered with everything I had carried for years.

As I began to write down my triggers and trace them back, patterns became clear in a way I could no longer ignore. Being interrupted, feeling overlooked, or sensing that I was not being valued carried an emotional weight that went far beyond the moment itself. Those reactions were not just about what was happening in front of me. They were connected to deeper wounds, to experiences that had shaped how I saw myself and how I believed others saw me. What looked like an overreaction on the surface was often an echo of something that had never been fully resolved.

Through that awareness, I began to learn how to slow myself down internally, how to deescalate my emotions before they took over, and how to choose not to react to everything impulsively.

Learning how the mind and body respond to perceived threats gave me a level of understanding I had never experienced before, and that understanding changed everything. I began to see that anger is not something that slowly builds with logic and intention, but something that can rise instantly, almost automatically, as if my body was reacting before my mind even had a chance to catch up. The intensity I felt in those moments was not random, and it was not a reflection of me being a bad person. It was a response, a conditioned reaction shaped by experiences that had taught me, consciously or not, to stay on guard.

That awareness did not excuse the way I had behaved in the past, but it gave me something I had been missing for most of my life, which was clarity. It allowed me to understand that I was not broken in the way I had once believed. There was nothing inherently wrong with me. What I was dealing with was unhealed pain and a lack of tools, a lack of guidance on how to process emotions that felt overwhelming and consuming. For the first time, I was being shown practical ways to calm myself down, to recognize what was happening internally, and to respond differently.

I am deeply grateful that I made the decision to walk into that anger management class, even though it was not something I ever imagined myself doing. That choice gave me access to understanding that I did not have before, and it opened my eyes to a truth that is hard but necessary to acknowledge. There are so many people whose lives have taken a completely different path because they never learned how to manage what they were feeling. There are people sitting in prison cells right now, not because they are inherently bad, but because they did not have the tools, the awareness, or the support to handle their emotions in moments that required something different.

As I continued to do the work, the changes did not happen all at once, and they did not come in a way that felt dramatic or overwhelming. Instead, they showed up slowly, almost quietly, in ways that felt steady and real. I began to notice that I could create space between what I felt and how I responded. That space, even when it was only a few seconds, became one of the most valuable tools I have ever developed. It gave me the ability to pause instead of react, to take a breath before allowing my emotions to take over, and to become aware of what was happening inside of me in a way I had never been before.

Breathing became more than just something my body did automatically. It became intentional. It became a way to ground myself in moments where everything inside of me wanted to react immediately.

In those pauses, I began to ask myself different questions. I started to look beyond the surface of the anger and consider what I was truly feeling underneath it. Was it hurt, fear, disappointment, or something deeper that had been triggered? I also began to question whether the situation in front of me truly required the level of intensity I was experiencing, or if I was responding to something much older that had been carried into the present moment.

That level of awareness did not make me perfect, and it did not mean I always got it right, but it gave me something I had never had before, which was choice. And with that choice, everything began to change in a way that felt not only possible, but sustainable. It created a new way of moving through life, one where I was no longer controlled by my immediate reactions, but guided by a deeper understanding of what was happening within me.

Looking back now, choosing to confront my anger stands out as one of the most empowering decisions I have ever made. It required me to release the identity I had built around being strong in that way, the version of strength that was rooted in reaction, defense, and control, and to accept a truth that felt unfamiliar at first. Real strength does not come from reacting. It comes from understanding. It comes from being willing to sit with what is uncomfortable, to take responsibility for your behavior, and to do the work necessary to change it in a way that is honest and lasting.

Many people never reach that point until something forces them to stop and take a closer look. Broken relationships, lost opportunities, and moments that cannot be undone often become the wake up call that makes everything painfully clear. I am deeply grateful that I chose to pause before my life was altered by a single moment I could not take back. Anger does not need time to create damage. It only takes one moment, one reaction, one decision made without awareness, for something to be said or done that cannot be undone.

What I came to understand is that anger is not a reliable protector. It does not build loving connections, it does not create lasting success in any form. It does not support your well being. It can take a toll on your body in ways that are often overlooked, showing up as stress, tension, and physical symptoms that seem unrelated but are deeply connected to what is happening internally. For me, that showed up in migraines and health issues that I treated on the surface without realizing the root was something much deeper.

Learning to pause, breathe and think became one of the most powerful practices I developed. Even a brief moment of awareness has the ability to change the direction of an interaction. Instead of reacting immediately, I began to ask myself what I was truly feeling, whether it was disappointment, fear, or something else entirely. Naming the emotion beneath the anger softened the reaction in a way that allowed me to respond differently.

When I reflect on my past now, I can see how experiences with loss, inconsistency, and disappointment shaped the way I reacted to people and situations. Those experiences left an imprint, and without understanding them, I carried that imprint into every area of my life. What I once believed was simply my strong Leo personality was actually a pattern that had been formed over time.

For a long time, I labeled myself as angry and broken, and I wore that identity as a form of protection. It kept people at a distance and allowed me to feel like I was in control, even when I was not. What I understand now is that anger is often a signal. It points to something that needs attention, something that needs to be understood, and something that is asking to be healed.

Every situation you face can be handled from a place of awareness if you are willing to do the internal work first. That does not mean you become passive or silent or allow others to take advantage of you. It means your response becomes intentional instead of reactive, grounded instead of impulsive, and aligned with who you truly are instead of what you have been through.

You are not destined to remain the version of yourself that was shaped by pain. Growth is possible, awareness is possible, and change is possible. I lived long enough believing that anger defined me, and I know what it feels like to carry that identity. Once I understood where it came from and took responsibility for how I responded, I began to move toward something different, a kinder more peaceful life.

Anger may explain parts of your story, but it does not have to write the rest of it.

3

You Are Not Your Anger

Most people do not realize when the shift begins to happen within them, when something they feel slowly turns into something they believe they are. Anger, which may have started as a reaction to certain moments, certain people, or certain experiences, begins to take on a different role over time. Instead of being something that rises and eventually passes, it becomes something you carry, something you claim, something that feels like it defines you. It moves from "I felt angry in that moment" to "this is just who I am," and once that belief settles in, it quietly starts shaping everything, from the way you respond to situations to the way people approach you before you even say a word.

That was me in my early twenties, and I can say that honestly now with a level of awareness I did not have back then. I told myself I was just sassy, just strong, just someone who did not take anything from anyone, but underneath that label was something much deeper that I was not ready to face. I was angry at the world for what I had been through, angry at God for allowing certain things to happen in my life, and carrying a level of hurt and disappointment that I had never fully processed. That anger did not just show up in certain moments, it became part of how I saw myself, part of how I introduced myself to others, and part of how I moved through the world.

For a long time, I spoke about myself in that way without hesitation. I would warn people about my temper as if I was doing them a favor, sometimes even laughing about it, presenting it as something that made me strong or made me real. There was a sense of pride in it, a belief that being that way meant I could not be taken advantage of, that I could not be hurt the way I had been hurt before. What I did not understand at the time was that every time I repeated those words, I was reinforcing something I had not taken the time to question. I was giving anger a permanent place in my identity, allowing it to stay exactly where it was without ever asking where it came from or what it was protecting.

What made that even more complicated is that anger created distance in a way that felt safe to me. It kept people from getting too close, and at the time, that felt necessary. Bonding with people meant opening myself up, and opening myself up meant risking loss, and loss was something I knew all too well. Somewhere deep inside, there was a fear that if I allowed myself to truly connect, I would eventually have to feel that kind of pain again. Anger became the barrier that made sure no one could get close enough to hurt me in that way. It felt like protection, but in reality, it was also preventing me from experiencing the kind of connection I needed.

Each time I leaned into that identity, it became more familiar, more comfortable, and more difficult to separate from who I actually was. I was not just expressing anger anymore, I was becoming it, and the longer I carried that belief, the more it shaped the way I experienced my life without me even realizing it.

Identity is powerful in ways that most people underestimate. The words you use to describe yourself begin to shape how you experience your life. What you repeat becomes familiar, and what becomes familiar eventually feels comfortable, even when it is not healthy for you. I had grown so used to reacting quickly, to speaking sharply, and to staying on edge that anything outside of that felt unnatural. Calmness felt foreign. Pausing before responding felt uncomfortable. Letting something go without reacting felt like weakness. Anger, on the other hand, felt predictable. It was something I knew how to access immediately, something that gave me a sense of control in moments where I felt anything but secure.

Living in that constant state of readiness takes a toll that is not always obvious at first. When anger becomes part of your identity, your body rarely relaxes. Your nervous system remains alert, scanning for anything that might resemble a threat, even when there is no real danger present. Situations that are neutral begin to feel personal. A tone of voice can sound like disrespect. A small mistake can feel intentional. You start reacting not just to what is happening, but to what it reminds you of, and without awareness, those reactions can begin to define the way you move through the world.

Looking back now, I can see how much of that was rooted in abandonment and the fear that came with it. Somewhere deep inside, there was a belief that I had to protect myself at all costs, that I could not afford to appear vulnerable, and that letting my guard down would lead to being hurt again. Anger became the shield I carried everywhere, a way of telling the world not to get too close, a way of maintaining distance so I would never have to experience that level of pain again. It felt strong, it felt protective, and for a long time, it felt necessary.

The problem with building your identity around anger is that it does not stay contained in one area of your life. It shows up everywhere. It shows up in your work, in your relationships, in your friendships, and in your role as a parent. You may believe you are simply being assertive or standing your ground, but the people around you often experience something very different. They feel tension, they feel unpredictability, and they begin to adjust their behavior around you in ways that create distance instead of connection.

I had to face that truth in my own life. The people around me were not just seeing a driven, hardworking woman. Some of them were experiencing someone whose reactions could shift quickly, someone who responded with intensity in moments that did not always require it. Even when I believed I was justified, I had to acknowledge that my responses were shaping the emotional environment around me in ways I had not intended.

There is a difference between having standards and reacting from a place of unhealed emotion. There is a difference between setting boundaries and allowing frustration to take over. For a long time, I blurred those lines, convincing myself that I was simply refusing to tolerate certain behaviors when in reality I was allowing old wounds to influence how I responded in the present.

Once anger becomes part of your identity, it becomes something you defend instead of something you question. You explain it, justify it, and protect it because letting it go would require you to look deeper, to ask uncomfortable questions, and to take responsibility for something that once felt automatic. That realization can be unsettling because it challenges everything you thought you knew about yourself.

I remember the moment I began to consider the possibility that I was not actually an angry person at my core. That thought did not bring immediate relief. It brought discomfort, because if anger was not simply who I was, then it meant I had learned it somewhere along the way. It meant it had been developed, reinforced, and repeated over time, and if that was true, then it also meant I had the responsibility to unlearn it.

Responsibility can feel heavy, but it is also where your power begins. If something is part of your personality, it feels permanent, like something you have to live with. When you begin to understand that it is a learned response, something shaped by experiences and repeated reactions, it opens the door for change. Patterns can be interrupted. Habits can be replaced. The brain is capable of adapting in ways that allow new responses to take root.

When I started looking at my own experiences honestly, I began to see how much unprocessed grief I had been carrying, how much fear had been sitting beneath the surface, and how much of my anger was actually sadness that I had never allowed myself to feel. That understanding did not excuse the way I had responded in the past, but it gave me clarity, and clarity created space for something different to begin.

You do not have to continue introducing yourself to yourself as an angry person. You do not have to accept that label as something permanent or unchangeable. There is a difference between feeling anger and becoming it, and that distinction matters more than most people realize. You are not your reactions. You are not your past responses. You are a person who has experienced things that shaped how you learned to protect yourself.

Letting go of that identity does not mean suppressing emotion or pretending you do not feel things deeply. It means creating separation between who you are and what you feel in a given moment. It means allowing yourself to recognize anger without allowing it to define you.

If you have carried that label for a long time, take a moment to question it instead of accepting it as truth. Labels have a way of settling into your sense of self, influencing how you see yourself and how you move through the world. Over time, they stop feeling like descriptions and start feeling like facts. Challenging that belief is where change begins.

No one is born angry at the world. Experiences shape you. Pain shapes you. Disappointment, fear, rejection, and instability can all contribute to the way you respond to life. Anger often becomes the expression that feels safest, because it feels stronger than sadness and more controlled than fear. It becomes a way to maintain a sense of power in moments where you once felt powerless.

Instead of judging yourself for the ways you have reacted, begin to approach those moments with curiosity. Think back to when you first remember feeling that intensity inside of you. Consider what was happening in your life at that time, what you were experiencing, and what you may not have had the ability to process fully. Tracing those patterns is not about placing blame. It is about understanding yourself in a way that allows growth to take place.

There is always a story behind the reaction, something that explains why the emotion feels as strong as it does. Anger often develops as a way to protect a version of you that did not feel safe, heard, or valued. That part of you may still be responding, even though the original situation has long passed.

When you begin to look beneath the surface, the intensity starts to make sense. It stops feeling random and starts feeling connected. That connection is what allows you to begin shifting how you respond, because once you understand the root, you are no longer reacting blindly.

You are not defined by your worst moments or your strongest reactions. You are defined by your willingness to grow, to reflect, and to choose something different when you know better. The version of you that once relied on anger to feel safe is not the only version that exists.

Anger may have served a purpose at one point in your life. It may have protected you when you needed protection. It may have created distance when closeness felt dangerous. Survival responses are not meant to become permanent identities. Once you reach a place where you can reflect, you also reach a place where you can choose.

You are allowed to evolve beyond the patterns that once defined you. You are allowed to separate your identity from your reactions. You are allowed to understand your past without allowing it to control your present.

Anger is something you feel.

It is not who you are.

4

The Holes You Didn't Know You Were Carrying

After keeping my personal story hidden for years, there came a point in my life where I finally allowed myself to speak honestly about what I had been through, and when I did, something unexpected began to unfold. I started to realize that my story was not as rare or as isolated as I once believed. There are so many people in this world quietly trying to heal from their own trauma, carrying experiences they have never fully spoken about or processed, holding onto pain in silence because they do not always feel safe enough to share it.

When I began speaking motivationally and opening up about my journey, I started to see that truth in a very real way. After I would come off stage, there would be long lines of people waiting, not just to speak, but to connect, to hug me, and to share pieces of their own stories. People would tell me about the trauma they had experienced, the pain they had carried for years, and the ways they had been trying to navigate life while holding onto so much internally. Those moments were deeply emotional, and they showed me something I could no longer ignore. I was not alone in what I had experienced, and neither were they.

That is when I knew my story was not just something I had lived through, it was something that could help others. It became clear that sharing it had purpose, and that is what led me to continue speaking, to pour into others through the #In59Seconds Movement, and to write self help books that reach people in moments where they may feel unseen or misunderstood.

Through those experiences, I began to understand just how many people are carrying pain from their past, often without realizing how much it is influencing their present. That realization shifted the way I saw people in a profound way. I no longer saw individuals only for who they appeared to be on the surface. I began to recognize something deeper, something that is not always visible at first glance.

I started to see adults carrying unhealed versions of themselves beneath the surface, abandoned children living inside grown bodies, people walking around with unresolved pain, reacting to present moments with emotions that did not belong to the present at all.

For so long, I believed that my anger meant something was wrong with me, that I was too much, too emotional, or somehow irreparably broken in a way that other people were not. That belief carried weight, and it shaped how I saw myself for years. I made me feel bad about who I was. But the more I began to share my story honestly, without hiding or minimizing it, the more that belief began to shift. I started to understand that I was not alone, and I was not defective. I was wounded, and so were many of the people around me.

There are so many individuals moving through life carrying pain they have never fully acknowledged, doing their best to function, to show up, and to maintain some sense of normalcy while something inside of them remains unresolved. They go to work, they raise families, they smile when they are supposed to, and from the outside everything can appear stable, yet internally something feels unsettled, something feels heavy, something feels like it has never truly been addressed. That internal unrest does not simply disappear because it is ignored or pushed aside. It finds ways to express itself, often through reactions that seem bigger than the moment, through defensiveness, emotional distance, or intensity that feels difficult to control.

When pain is left unhealed for too long, it does not just stay contained within a person. It begins to surface in ways that can affect not only their life, but the lives of others around them. In some cases, it shows up in quiet ways, through strained relationships, broken communication, or emotional withdrawal. In more serious situations, when that pain reaches a level that feels overwhelming and unmanageable, it can lead to moments where people lose control in ways that are deeply tragic and life altering.

We see it in the world around us more often than we would like to admit. Stories of individuals reaching a breaking point, situations where emotions that were never understood or processed turn into actions that cannot be undone. It can show up in acts of violence, in families being torn apart, in lives being lost, and in moments where someone feels so overwhelmed that they believe there is no other way out. These situations are heartbreaking, and they remind us of how serious it is when emotional pain is left unaddressed for too long.

Speaking about this is not about excusing harmful behavior, and it is not about minimizing the impact of those actions. It is about acknowledging that there is often something deeper beneath the surface, something that was never healed, never understood, and never given the attention it needed. It is about recognizing that emotional pain, when ignored, can grow into something much larger than the original experience.

At the same time, there is another truth that matters just as much. Healing is possible. Learning how to regulate your emotions is possible. Understanding yourself in a deeper way is possible. It requires willingness. It requires honesty. It requires a decision to face what has been carried instead of continuing to push it aside. That process is not always easy, but it is necessary if we want to change the direction of our lives and the impact we have on others.

I did not begin doing that work until much later in my life, well into my thirties, and that is a long time to move through the world reacting from wounds that had never been fully examined. Looking back, I can see how much of my life was lived on autopilot, responding instead of understanding, protecting instead of healing. My hope in sharing this is that someone else does not have to wait as long as I did to begin that process, because healing does not need to be delayed until after relationships have been damaged, opportunities have been lost, and peace has been disrupted.

The way I understand it now is through something I call emotional holes. These are not visible to anyone else, and they are not something you can point to physically, yet their presence is undeniable once you become aware of them. They are created through experiences that were never fully processed, through rejection, abandonment, loss, neglect, and moments where something essential was taken or never given. They leave behind gaps in the way you feel, the way you perceive yourself, and the way you interact with others, shaping your responses in ways that are not always obvious at first.

For years, I carried those holes without realizing what they were. I only knew that I felt things deeply, reacted quickly, and often found myself dealing with the aftermath of emotions that seemed much larger than the situation itself. At the time, I did not understand where those reactions were coming from, and I did not question them in a way that led to clarity. As I became more aware, I started noticing that this was not unique to me. So many people were living with similar wounds, some deeper than others, some hidden more carefully, and others expressed openly through anger, sarcasm, emotional distance, or defensiveness.

Life has a way of continuing forward whether you are ready or not, and in that movement, it is easy to go on living without recognizing that these wounds are even there. We continue showing up, handling responsibilities, building relationships, and doing what is expected of us, all while carrying unseen scars that have quietly shaped the way we think, feel, and respond. Those wounds do not just affect us internally. They influence every interaction, every relationship, and every connection we have, often without us even realizing it. They interfere with our ability to give and receive love in the way God intended. We were created to love naturally, wholeheartedly, and without fear, but when love is denied, inconsistent, or taken away at critical moments in our lives, something begins to form within us.

Those holes do not remain the same size. When they are left unaddressed, when they are not acknowledged or healed, they grow. Life continues to move forward, responsibilities increase, relationships form, and on the surface everything can appear stable and even successful, yet internally those openings begin to expand. The unattended holes in our hearts get bigger. They begin to influence how we interpret simple interactions. They prevent us from giving and receiving love the way God intended for it to be. We were born to love naturally, wholeheartedly and without fear, but when we have been denied love from the beginning of our lives ,holes form in our hearts. What should feel safe begins to feel uncertain, because early experiences have shaped your understanding of connection in ways that are rooted in fear rather than trust.

I personally believe that small pieces of our soul escape through those holes, and we spend much of our lives trying to retrieve them, trying to piece ourselves back together again without fully understanding what we are searching for. In that process, we can hurt other people, sometimes without any intention of doing so. There were times in my life when I had no idea why I reacted so explosively to certain situations. I was not trying to hurt anyone, but I was responding from a place of pain that I did not fully understand.

There were moments when it truly felt like pieces of me were missing, like something had slipped away over the years and I was constantly trying to get it back without even realizing that was what I was doing. Every time I overreacted to something that felt like rejection, every time I tried to control a situation so I would not feel abandoned again, I was responding from those unseen wounds. In the process, I hurt people who had no intention of hurting me, but at the time, I could not see beyond my own pain.

The people closest to me did not fully understand it either. From their perspective, it often looked like I was just being a hot head, someone who overreacted, someone whose emotions seemed unpredictable and intense. There were moments where my reactions confused even the people who knew me best, because the level of intensity did not match what was actually happening in front of us. What none of us understood at the time was that those reactions were not coming from the present moment alone. They were layered with years of unresolved pain and emotion, surfacing through situations that only appeared small on the surface, but were connected to something much deeper within me.

One moment that stands out clearly happened during a simple outing at the mall. My ex-husband made a casual comment about liking a pair of shoes on a woman who walked past us. There was no disrespect in his tone, no hidden meaning behind his words, and no intention to hurt me in any way. He meant no harm whatsoever. It was a simple observation, something that, in a healthy emotional space, would have passed without a second thought and held no weight at all.

But that is not how I experienced it in that moment. Instead, something inside of me took those words and translated them into something entirely different. I did not hear appreciation for a pair of shoes. I heard that I was not enough. I heard comparison. I heard rejection in a moment where none actually existed. The reaction that followed had nothing to do with what he said and everything to do with what I had been carrying inside of me for years.

What happened next had nothing to do with shoes. It was a response rooted in my own insecurities, fears, and unhealed wounds that had been building beneath the surface long before that moment ever happened. I went home, gathered every pair of shoes I owned, and threw them at him, completely overwhelmed by emotions that felt real and intense in that moment. I truly believed what I was feeling. I convinced myself that he wanted someone else, that I was not attractive enough, that I was somehow lacking in ways I could not measure or fix. None of that was true.

His comment did not mean any of those things. He simply liked the shoes the woman had on, and that was the full extent of it. The meaning I attached to it came from somewhere much deeper, from beliefs I had formed over time about myself, about my worth, and about how I thought others saw me.

Looking back now, I can see that moment with a completely different level of awareness. There is even a sense of understanding and, at times, a little humor when I think about how far removed my reaction was from the actual situation. At the time, though, it was intense and painful, and I believed I was defending myself.

In reality, I was reacting to something much deeper and older than that particular moment, something that had nothing to do with him and everything to do with what I had not yet healed within myself yet.

Growing up without the presence of a mother left a mark that I did not fully understand until much later. Even though I had people in my life who loved me, I did not know how to fully receive that love because I had not yet learned how to see myself as worthy of it. Until those wounds were acknowledged, every relationship I entered carried the risk of being filtered through fear instead of trust.

Another moment that remains clear in my memory takes me back to when I was eighteen, still grieving the loss of my grandmother, trying to find my footing in a life that felt uncertain without her. My sister had gone away to college, and when she told me she would not be coming home for the holidays, the reaction that surfaced in me was overwhelming. We didn't have a lot of family left and I was still in a very fragile state..From a logical perspective, her decision made sense, she was building her life, adjusting to something new, but emotionally it felt like another loss, another confirmation that I was being left behind.

I cried, I reacted, I expressed emotions that were much bigger than the situation itself, because what I was feeling was not just about that moment. It was connected to a deeper fear of abandonment, one that had been shaped by experiences long before that conversation. At the time, I could not separate the two. All I knew was that I felt alone and hurt in a way that felt familiar.

It took years for me to understand that those reactions were not random. They were connected to beliefs I had formed about myself, beliefs that told me I was not valuable enough to be chosen, not important enough to be stayed for. That belief influenced more than I realized, shaping how I responded to people and situations without me even being aware of it.

Nothing truly begins to change until you are willing to acknowledge what you have been carrying. Physical wounds have a way of healing over time, but emotional wounds require attention. They do not simply disappear because time has passed. In many cases, they become more deeply rooted, especially when they are repeatedly triggered without being addressed.

If you are reading this and recognizing pieces of yourself in these experiences, take a moment to consider what your own emotional wounds might be. They may come from different circumstances, different experiences, but the impact often looks similar. Sensitivity, defensiveness, emotional reactions that feel difficult to control, or a tendency to withdraw when things feel overwhelming.

The process of healing those wounds is not about weakness. It requires honesty, courage, and a willingness to look at parts of yourself that may feel uncomfortable. For some, that means therapy. For others, it may mean writing, reflection, or having conversations that bring clarity and release. The method may vary, but the intention remains the same, to understand what has been left unhealed and to begin closing those gaps.

At one point in my life, I believed that closure would come from other people, from apologies, from acknowledgment, from things being said in a way that would finally make everything feel resolved. What I came to understand is that healing does not depend on someone else showing up the way you hope they will. It is something you create within yourself.

Forgiveness became a turning point in that process for me. It was not about excusing what had happened, but about releasing the hold it had on me. As I worked through that, something began to shift. The weight I had been carrying started to feel lighter, and the reactions that once felt automatic began to soften.

When you begin to understand that your reactions may be connected to something deeper, you gain a level of awareness that changes everything. Instead of only focusing on what is happening around you, you begin to look inward and ask what is being activated within you. That question creates space, and in that space, change becomes possible.

Healing is not immediate, and it does not happen all at once. It requires patience, consistency, and a willingness to stay present with yourself in ways that may feel unfamiliar at first. The outcome, however, is something that reaches far beyond you. As you begin to heal, the way you interact with others changes, the way you respond to situations shifts, and the energy you bring into your relationships becomes more grounded and more intentional.

The world around us reflects so much unprocessed pain, and when individuals begin to do the work within themselves, that impact extends outward in ways that are more powerful than we often realize. When you begin to close the wounds you have been carrying, you are not only changing your own life, you are changing the way you show up in the lives of others.

The intensity that once lived inside of me did not disappear on its own. It softened because I was willing to do the work needed on myself and look at what had been broken and attempt to understand it, and to take responsibility for how I moved forward. That same possibility exists for you, not because your story is the same as mine, but because healing is available to anyone willing to face what they have been carrying and choose something different.

5

You Are Not Too Far Gone

There is a part of you that may already be reading this with hesitation, a quiet voice inside that says, this might not be for me, because you have seen your own reactions, you have felt the intensity of your emotions, and maybe you have moments in life that you wish you could take back. You might remember the times when your screamed louder than you intended, when your words came out harsh and sharper than you meant them to, when your reactions created distance between you and the people you care about, and somewhere along the way, you may have started to believe that this is just who you are. That belief can feel heavy, especially when it has been reinforced over time by labels, by experiences, and by the way people respond to you. Life does not have to be that way. Relationships can be re-built.

I want you to hear this clearly, not just as words on a page, but as something you allow yourself to truly consider. You are not too far gone. You are not beyond change. You are not destined to be the person everyone has to tiptoe around, the one people hesitate to speak honestly with because they are afraid of how you might respond. Those moments you have had do not define the totality of who you are, even if they have felt loud and overwhelming at times. They are reflections of something deeper, something that has not been fully understood or fully healed. Love heals and it is never too late to learn to lead with love.

When you have been through loss, betrayal, disappointment, or trauma that shook you to your core, your mind and your body learn how to protect you in the only ways they know how. You may have experienced things that no one prepared you for, things that altered the way you see the world and the way you see yourself. There are people walking through life carrying the weight of death, of abandonment, of physical violation, of broken trust, of moments that changed everything in an instant. Those experiences do not simply disappear because time has passed. They settle into your nervous system, into your thoughts, into your reactions, and they begin to show up in ways that may not always make sense on the surface.

You may have believed at some point that confronting someone, telling them exactly how they hurt you, or even releasing your anger in a moment of intensity would bring you relief. It can feel like power in the moment, like you are finally standing up for yourself, finally being heard, finally making sure no one ever disrespects you again. The truth is that those moments rarely bring the kind of peace you are looking for. When everything settles, when the emotions come back down, there is often a feeling that lingers, a quiet awareness that something about that reaction did not align with who you truly are.

There were moments in my own life when I thought I was being strong by reacting the way I did, moments when I believed that setting someone straight or making my point in an explosive way meant that I was protecting myself. I convinced myself that if I did not respond that way, people would take advantage of me, that I would be seen as weak, or that I would be overlooked. What I did not understand at the time was that those reactions were never coming from the strongest part of me. They were coming from a place that had been deeply hurt, a place that had never been given the space to heal.

If you think back to the earlier chapters, you already know that my life was shaped by experiences that left a lasting impact. Losing my father at a young age, being abandoned by my mother, and most significantly, witnessing the violent loss of my grandmother, the woman who raised me and loved me when I needed it most, created a level of pain that I did not know how to process. That moment did not just take her from me, it disrupted something inside of me that I carried for years without understanding. The world may have seen certain behaviors and labeled them as mean, but what was really there was a heart that had been deeply affected by trauma, a heart that did not know how to make sense of what it had experienced.

That is something I want you to understand about yourself as well. No one is born mean. No one enters this world with the intention of hurting others or pushing people away. What develops over time are protective layers, ways of responding that are built from experiences that felt overwhelming, confusing, or painful. Those layers can become so strong that they begin to look like personality traits, but underneath them is still the core of who you are, and that core is not defined by anger.

There is a reason your reactions feel as intense as they do, and that reason deserves your attention, not your judgment. When you begin to look at yourself with curiosity instead of criticism, something shifts. Instead of asking what is wrong with me, you begin asking what happened to me, and that question opens a completely different door. It allows you to see that your responses did not come from nowhere, they came from somewhere that has been asking to be understood for a long time.

Seeking help for yourself is not a sign that something is wrong with you. It is a sign that you are ready to understand yourself in a deeper way. Personal development, therapy, coaching, reflection, whatever path you choose, those are tools that help you uncover what has been hidden beneath the surface. They give you language for what you have been feeling and strategies for responding differently when those emotions rise.

There is also an important truth that needs to be acknowledged, and that is the difference between release and healing. Exploding on someone may feel like release in the moment, but it does not heal the source of what you are feeling. Confronting someone may feel like it will bring closure, but if your healing is dependent on how they respond, you are placing your peace in someone else's hands. True healing happens when you take that responsibility back and begin doing the work within yourself, regardless of whether someone else acknowledges your pain.

You are allowed to want better for yourself. You are allowed to grow beyond the patterns that once defined you. You are allowed to become someone who responds with intention instead of reacting from pain. That does not mean you will never feel anger again, and it does not mean you will always get it right. What it means is that you are no longer letting those moments define who you are or control how you move through your life.

There is a version of you that exists beyond the reactions, beyond the labels, beyond the moments you regret, and that version of you is still there, waiting to be recognized. The work is not about becoming someone else. It is about returning to who you were before the pain shaped your responses in ways you did not understand.

You do not have to carry the weight of being labeled as the one who always explodes, the one people are careful around, or the one who is seen as difficult. You have the ability to change the way you show up, to rebuild trust within yourself, and to create a different experience in your relationships.

Give yourself permission to begin that process without judgment. Allow yourself to be a work in progress. Understand that healing is not about perfection, it is about awareness, intention, and consistency. The fact that you are here, reading this, reflecting on your own experiences, already means something is shifting.

You are not too far gone.

You are just beginning to understand.

6

You're Right Doesn't Mean You're Right

One of the hardest truths you will ever have to accept on your journey is this, being justified in your anger does not give you permission to lose control. That realization does not come easily, and when it finally lands, it can feel humbling in a way that forces you to look at yourself without making excuses. There are moments in your life where someone will disrespect you, lie to you, disappoint you, or cross a line that should never have been crossed, and in those moments, your anger can feel completely valid. In many cases, it is valid. What you feel makes sense. What you experienced may have been wrong. The part that changes everything is understanding that just because your anger is understandable does not mean your reaction is wise.

There is a difference between feeling anger and acting from it, and that difference will determine the direction of your life more than you may realize right now. Anger itself is not the enemy. It is a signal that something within you has been touched, something that feels unfair, painful, or out of alignment. The problem begins when you allow that signal to take control of your actions. When anger moves from something you feel into something that leads your behavior, the outcome rarely brings the peace or resolution you were hoping for. It may feel powerful in the moment, but when everything settles, you are often left with consequences that do not match the temporary release you experienced.

If you take a moment to reflect on your own life, you may begin to see how often your reactions have been shaped by more than just what was happening in front of you. When someone says something that feels disrespectful, the reaction that rises within you is not always just about that moment. It can be connected to every time you have felt dismissed, overlooked, or devalued in your life. When someone challenges you, it may not just feel like a disagreement. It may feel like a threat to your sense of control or your sense of worth. What is happening in the present is often layered with everything you have carried from the past, and without awareness, those layers can take over completely.

Understanding this does not mean you excuse the behavior of others. People will still say things that hurt. They will still make mistakes. They will still act in ways that are inconsiderate or wrong. The point is not to pretend that those moments do not matter. The point is to separate what happened from how you choose to respond to it. That separation is where your power lives.

Responsibility is the turning point, and it is not always comfortable to step into. You may find yourself asking why you have to be the one to do the work when someone else caused the pain in the first place. That question is real, and it deserves to be acknowledged, but the answer is even more important. Your healing is not about what they did. It is about what you choose to do next. Holding on to uncontrolled anger does not punish the person who hurt you. It extends the impact of that moment into every area of your life long after it has passed.

There are people whose entire lives have changed in a single moment because they reacted without pausing. Some are sitting behind bars right now because of a quick decision they cannot take back. Relationships have ended, opportunities have disappeared, and entire life paths have shifted permanently because one reaction was allowed to take over without thought. It does not take much for that to happen. It only takes one moment where emotion overrides awareness.

Anger is not your friend. On the contrary, it can become the worst enemy you have ever known.

Aside from pushing away people who truly care about you, anger can and will create severe emotional, mental, and even physical distress over time. No matter how provoked you may feel, there is always a moment available to you, even if it is brief, where you can pause, take a breath, and assess what is happening before responding. That pause matters more than you may realize. Giving yourself even a second to think about the possible outcome of your reaction can prevent damage that cannot be undone. Rarely has anything truly productive come from responding out of anger, and more often than not, it leads to hurt, regret, and unnecessary distance in relationships that matter. I experienced this firsthand in a way that forced me to confront it.

Running my business became overwhelming at times because I depended on others to perform at the level of excellence and consistency that I held myself to. Over the years, many different personalities came through my doors, each bringing their own habits, work ethic, and level of commitment. There was a constant pressure to maintain the quality that I had built from the ground up, starting in my own home long before I ever opened my salon. I learned very quickly that it is difficult to make other people care about something in the same way you do.

One day, I held a staff meeting with nine of my employees to address ongoing issues like tardiness, hygiene, and customer service. My intention was to speak generally, to address everything without singling anyone out, but one particular employee kept interrupting, asking over and over again if I was talking about her. My patience was already thin from constantly having to smooth things over with clients when mistakes were made, offering apologies and discounts to maintain the reputation of my business. It was my name on the building, and every mistake reflected back on me, which made those moments feel even more intense.

Her refusal to just listen and accept the general feedback frustrated me deeply, especially because she was often the one contributing to the very issues I was addressing. The more she spoke, the more I felt something rising inside of me, something familiar, something intense.

If you have ever heard someone describe seeing red, you will understand what I experienced in that moment. My vision shifted, and everything around me seemed to fade except for her face, which felt like it was right in front of me illuminated in red, smirking and provoking me. I reached for a small figurine on my desk and made a motion as if I was going to throw it at her. suddenly I stopped in my tracks. I sat back down in my chair, took a deep breath, and in that moment realized how quickly everything I had worked so hard for could have been taken away in a single, uncontrolled reaction. That awareness hit me immediately. I calmed myself down just enough to respond differently and told her, calmly, that she was fired.

That moment changed the direction of my life. I knew right then that I had a problem that needed to be addressed. No matter how frustrated I felt, no matter how justified I believed my emotions were, it was never acceptable to even consider harming someone, especially over something that could have been handled differently. That realization led me to seek the help I needed.

In a moment of honesty and desperation to get control over my emotions, I found an anger management coach named Dr. Young. He typically worked with court ordered clients, but we agreed to six weeks of one on one sessions. That decision opened a door that I had never walked through before.

I completed those sessions and went on to enroll in another anger management class at West LA College. Through that process, I began to learn about triggers, how to identify them, and how to manage them before they took over. I started to understand that my reactions were not random, that they were connected to deeper experiences and compounded by stress, especially from running my business.

For the first time, I understood something that changed everything. No matter the cause, no matter the history behind it, I was still responsible for my own reaction.

The next time you find yourself feeling angry or out of control, give yourself permission to slow down. Take a breath. Think about what you are about to say or do before you act on it. That small pause can prevent reactions that you may regret later. When anger takes over completely, it can lead to behavior that does not reflect who you truly are. those impulsive behaviors and destroy life as you know it.

Because I made the decision to change, I have been able to identify the things that trigger me and actively work to avoid falling into those same patterns again. I never want to feel as out of control as I did in that moment again.

As your awareness grows, something begins to shift in the way you approach those intense situations. Instead of focusing on whether you are right, you begin to consider what your reaction will create. That question alone has the power to change everything. Being right loses its value if the outcome leads to damage that cannot be repaired.

Learning to pause becomes one of the most valuable skills you can develop. It is not about ignoring your emotions or pretending they are not there. It is about creating a space between what you feel and how you respond. Even a few seconds of awareness can redirect an entire situation. A breath, a step back, or a decision to wait before responding can completely change the outcome.

There is a quiet strength in acknowledging your emotions without allowing them to control you. Recognizing that you are upset without projecting that feeling outward creates a level of control that is rooted in awareness rather than force. The way you communicate, your tone, your timing, and your presence all determine whether a situation escalates or resolves.

At first, responding differently did not feel natural to me at all. It required patience, intention, and a willingness to break patterns that had been deeply ingrained over time. Gradually, I began to notice changes, not just within myself, but in how others responded to me. When I spoke calmly, people listened differently. When I responded with clarity instead of intensity, communication improved. Respect was no longer based on fear, but on consistency and presence.

That same shift extends into every area of your life. When you choose steadiness over reaction, your relationships begin to change. You create space for healthier interactions, for better communication, and for deeper understanding. The people around you will still have their own challenges, but you are no longer contributing to the chaos.

Life will always present situations that test your patience. There will always be people who do not meet your expectations. The goal is not to eliminate anger completely. The goal is to reach a place where anger no longer controls how you show up in those moments.

If you have spent years identifying as someone with a short temper or intense reactions, understand that this is not who you are at your core. It is a pattern that has been repeated, and patterns can be changed. With awareness and consistency, new patterns can take their place.

You are allowed to feel what you feel. Your emotions are valid, and your experiences matter. At the same time, you are not required to let those emotions dictate your behavior. There is a powerful sense of control that comes from recognizing that you have a choice, even in the most intense moments.

Taking responsibility for your reactions is not about blaming yourself. It is about reclaiming your power. It means you are no longer at the mercy of your triggers. It means you are no longer allowing your past to control your present in ways that create more damage.

There is a difference between being powerful and being reactive. Once you understand that difference, everything begins to change.

Just because you are right does not mean your reaction is right, and learning that may be one of the most important steps you ever take toward becoming the version of yourself you were always meant to be.

7

What You See in Others Is Asking to Be Healed Within You

Some truths can feel uncomfortable at first, especially the ones that ask you to look at yourself in a way that goes deeper than what you may be used to. One of those truths is this. The things that irritate you the most in other people, the behaviors that make you tense, and the personalities that you instantly reject are often connected to something within you that is asking for your attention. That does not mean you are exactly like them in every way, and it does not mean you are wrong for noticing certain behaviors. What it does mean is that something is being reflected back to you, something that is touching a place inside of you that may not yet be fully healed, fully understood, or fully accepted.

That realization is not meant to make you feel bad about yourself. It is actually a positive and humbling place to grow from, because you cannot change what you refuse to acknowledge. Every person is a work in progress, and part of that growth comes from being willing to look inward when something external creates a strong reaction within you. Instead of immediately focusing on what is wrong with the other person, there is an opportunity to pause and become curious about what is happening inside of you. why are you so bothered by them?

There will be moments when someone affects you in a way that feels intense and difficult to explain. It may be a coworker who seems to get under your skin without saying much at all, a family member whose presence alone creates tension, or even a complete stranger whose energy feels unsettling. In those moments, it is easy to believe that the issue exists entirely within them, that they are simply negative, difficult, or unpleasant. While it is true that some people are carrying heavy energy, there is also something deeper available for you to explore within yourself.

When that feeling rises, give yourself a moment to pause instead of reacting immediately. Ask yourself a different question than you may be used to asking. Instead of focusing only on them, ask yourself why this person is affecting you so strongly and what that reaction might be revealing about you. That question is where growth begins, because it shifts your focus from judgment to awareness.

Sometimes the answer will not come right away, and that is okay. What matters is that you are willing to ask the question at all. There is something powerful about understanding that not every encounter is random. Certain people cross your path for a reason, and even the ones who challenge you the most can reveal something meaningful about your own journey. They can show you where you are still healing, where you are still growing, and where you are being called to evolve into the person God created you to be.

When you begin to approach life from that perspective, even the most frustrating interactions take on a different meaning. They are no longer just moments of irritation. They become opportunities for awareness, for growth, and for a deeper understanding of yourself.

That question requires honesty, and it requires a level of self awareness that not everyone is ready to step into right away. It is much easier to place all of the focus outward, to label someone else as the problem, and to move on without reflection. Growth begins when you are willing to pause and consider that your reaction may be connected to something internal, something that has been shaped by your own experiences, your own pain, and your own beliefs about yourself and the world around you.

There are characteristics you may see in others that you have rejected within yourself, traits that you have judged, suppressed, or tried to distance yourself from because they do not align with how you want to be seen. When those same traits appear in someone else, they can trigger a reaction that feels immediate and intense, not because of who they are alone, but because of what they represent to you on a deeper level. That does not mean you are that person, but it does mean there is something within you that is being called to your attention.

This is where personal development and transformation begin to take on a different meaning. It is not just about improving what is visible on the surface. It is about becoming aware of what exists beneath it, the patterns, the beliefs, and the emotional responses that influence how you experience the world. Accepting that you may see parts of yourself reflected in others is not easy, but it is one of the most freeing realizations you can have because it gives you the opportunity to grow in a way that is rooted in truth instead of avoidance.

At the same time, there is another layer to this that is important to acknowledge. Energy is real. You can feel it even when nothing is being said. A child can sense it. A baby can respond to it. There are moments where you walk into a room and feel a shift without anyone speaking a word. That awareness is valid. There are people who carry unresolved pain so deeply that it shows up in the way they move, the way they speak, and the way they interact with others. That energy can feel heavy, and your sensitivity to it does not mean something is wrong with you.

What it does mean is that there is something within them that has not yet been healed.

When you begin to see people through that lens, something starts to soften within you. Instead of immediately judging or rejecting them, you begin to recognize that their behavior is not the full expression of who they are. It is a reflection of what they have experienced, what they have carried, and what they may not yet know how to process. Just as your reactions were shaped by your past, theirs are shaped by theirs.

It is easy to forget that every person you encounter is on their own journey, navigating their own experiences, their own losses, and their own moments of confusion and pain. No one enters this world mean, negative, or broken at their core. Those traits are developed over time as a result of what has been experienced and how those experiences were interpreted. God did not create you or anyone else to be defined by negativity or harshness. Those are layers that have been built, not the truth of who someone is at their foundation.

When you begin to understand that, it becomes easier to respond with compassion instead of resistance. That does not mean you allow people to mistreat you or cross your boundaries. It means you see them clearly without reducing them to their behavior. It means you recognize that what you are witnessing is not the whole story.

There is something powerful about choosing to meet someone with kindness when your first instinct might be to pull away. Offering a smile, a kind word, or even a moment of patience can shift the energy of an interaction in ways that are not always visible but are always felt. You may never know what someone is carrying or how close they are to breaking under the weight of it. That small moment of kindness can reach them in a way you may never fully understand.

Even something as simple as choosing to greet someone you normally avoid, or softening your tone in a conversation that could easily become tense, creates a different experience not just for them, but for you as well. It interrupts the pattern. It shifts the dynamic. It reminds you that you have the ability to choose how you show up, regardless of what you are receiving.

There is also something deeply healing about recognizing that the parts of yourself you may have judged or rejected are not things to be pushed away, but things to be understood. When you bring awareness to those parts, when you allow yourself to explore where they came from and why they exist, they begin to lose their intensity. They no longer need to be projected outward because they are being acknowledged within.

The person you struggle with the most may be reflecting something you have not yet made peace with, and while that realization can feel uncomfortable, it is also an invitation. It is an invitation to grow, to understand yourself more deeply, and to release the judgment that keeps you disconnected from both yourself and others.

You do not have to carry the weight of constant irritation, frustration, or judgment toward the people around you. There is another way to experience those interactions, one that is rooted in awareness, compassion, and a deeper understanding of what it means to be human.

The next time you encounter someone who triggers something within you, pause for a moment before reacting. Take a breath and allow yourself to consider that what you are feeling may be pointing you toward something within yourself that is ready to be healed. At the same time, allow space for the possibility that they, too, are carrying something they have not yet learned how to release.

When you begin to see people in this way, the world starts to feel different. It becomes less about separation and more about understanding. Less about judgment and more about awareness. Less about reacting and more about choosing how you want to show up in each moment.

There is a level of peace that comes from releasing the need to define people by their worst moments and allowing yourself to see beyond what is immediately visible. That peace is not just something you give to others. It is something you give to yourself.

In that space, something within you begins to soften, something that allows you to move through the world with a sense of connection that is no longer blocked by the walls that once felt necessary to protect you.

8

When You Finally See Yourself Clearly

There comes a moment in your life when something shifts quietly but powerfully, a moment where you stop focusing only on what other people are doing and begin to see yourself with a level of honesty that you may have avoided for a long time. That moment does not always feel comfortable. In fact, it can feel unsettling, because it requires you to acknowledge parts of yourself that you once justified, ignored, or explained away.

Up until that point, it may have been easier to point outward, to identify what other people were doing wrong, how they spoke to you, how they treated you, and how their behavior made you feel. That perspective feels natural, especially when you have experienced real pain, real disappointment, and real moments where people did not show up the way they should have. What begins to change is the realization that while those experiences mattered, they are not the only thing shaping your life.

There is a deeper level of awareness that begins to emerge when you are willing to ask yourself a different kind of question, not just why did they do that, but why did that affect me the way it did. That question is not about blame. It is about understanding. It is about recognizing that your reactions are not random, and they are not just about the moment in front of you. They are connected to something that has been building over time, something that has roots in experiences you may not have fully processed.

Seeing yourself clearly does not mean judging yourself harshly or labeling yourself in a negative way. It means becoming aware of the patterns that have been running in the background, the habits of thought and behavior that have shaped how you respond to life. It means recognizing when your reactions are coming from a place of protection instead of a place of presence.

There is a level of maturity that comes with this kind of awareness, and it is not something that happens overnight. It develops gradually, through reflection, through honesty, and through a willingness to look at yourself without defensiveness. It requires you to acknowledge that some of the ways you have responded in the past may not align with who you truly are at your core.

You may begin to see moments differently, moments where you reacted strongly, moments where your words created distance, moments where your behavior may have hurt someone else even if that was never your intention. That awareness is not meant to create shame. It is meant to create understanding. It is meant to give you the opportunity to respond differently moving forward.

The version of you that reacted in those moments was doing the best it could with the awareness it had at the time. That does not mean you stay there. It means you grow from there. It means you take what you are beginning to understand and use it to create something better, something more aligned with who you are becoming.

There is strength in being able to say, I see it now. I understand it now. I am ready to do something different.

That moment of clarity is not the end of the process. It is the beginning of it.

9

You Don't Have to Be That Person Anymore

There is a version of you that people may have come to expect, a version that reacts quickly, speaks sharply, or carries an intensity that others have learned to navigate carefully. Over time, that version can begin to feel permanent, as if it is simply who you are and who you will always be. You may have heard it from others, or even said it to yourself, that you have a temper, that you are just direct, that you do not tolerate certain things, and while there may be truth in those statements, they do not tell the whole story.

The truth is that you do not have to continue being that version of yourself.

You are not locked into the patterns you developed during the most difficult moments of your life. You are not required to carry the same reactions into every situation, and you are not defined by the ways you responded when you were operating from pain instead of understanding. Those patterns may feel familiar, but familiarity does not mean permanence.

There is something incredibly freeing about realizing that change is available to you, not in a way that requires you to become someone completely different, but in a way that allows you to return to who you were before those patterns took hold. The core of who you are has not been lost. It has simply been covered by experiences that shaped how you learned to protect yourself.

Letting go of that version of yourself can feel uncomfortable at first, because it means stepping into something unfamiliar. It means responding in ways that may not feel natural yet, choosing calm when you are used to intensity, choosing reflection when you are used to reaction, and choosing understanding when you are used to defensiveness. That shift takes practice, and it takes patience.

There may be moments where you feel the old reactions rising within you, moments where everything in you wants to respond the way you always have. Those moments are not failures. They are opportunities. They are reminders that you are in the process of change, and change does not happen all at once.

Each time you pause instead of reacting, each time you choose your words with intention, each time you respond from a place of awareness instead of impulse, you are reinforcing a new pattern. Over time, those small choices begin to reshape how you experience your life.

You are allowed to outgrow the version of yourself that was shaped by pain. You are allowed to evolve beyond the identity that was formed in moments where you were trying to protect yourself. You are allowed to become someone who responds with clarity, with intention, and with a sense of control that comes from understanding rather than force.

The person you have been does not have to be the person you continue to be.

You get to choose something different.

10

Healing Changes Everything

As I got older healing stopped being something I thought about and became something I begin to live daily. The same can be true for you. Allow healing to move from an idea into an real experience, something that shows up in the way you think, the way you respond, and the way you move through your life on a daily basis. That shift does not happen all at once. It unfolds gradually, in moments where you begin to notice that something feels different within you.

You may notice that situations that once triggered you no longer have the same intensity. You don't cry as much or get your feelings hurt as regular as you used to. You may find that you are able to pause and think where you once reacted immediately. You may begin to feel a sense of calm in places where there used to be tension. Those changes may seem small at first, but they are significant, because they reflect something deeper that is taking place within you. They reflect personal transformation and healing.

Healing does not erase what you have been through. It changes how you carry it. The experiences that once felt overwhelming begin to feel more manageable. The emotions that once felt uncontrollable begin to feel more understood. The patterns that once felt automatic begin to feel like conscious choices, and in that shift, you begin to reclaim a sense of control over your life that may have felt out of reach before.

There is a beautiful softness that begins to settle into your life when you start healing in a real and honest way, a kind of gentleness that changes how you see yourself and how you begin to see the people around you. The same things that once triggered you so quickly begin to feel different, not because life has suddenly become perfect, but because you are no longer looking at everything through the same lens. You start to recognize that people are more than their worst moments, just as you are more than yours, and that realization alone creates space where there used to be tension. It allows you to breathe in situations where you once felt tight, to observe instead of immediately reacting, and to understand that behavior is often just the surface of something much deeper that has not yet been healed.

Moving through life with that awareness does not make you weak, and it does not mean you accept things that go against your peace. There is strength in responding with intention instead of impulse, in choosing your words instead of letting them spill out of emotion, and in standing firm in your boundaries without losing yourself in the process. A different kind of power begins to develop within you, one that is not loud or reactive, but steady, grounded, and deeply rooted in understanding. It shows up in the way you carry yourself, in the way you handle conflict, and in the way you no longer feel the need to prove anything through force or intensity.

With that growth comes a deeper sense of responsibility, not the kind that weighs you down, but the kind that reminds you that your life is still yours to shape. The way you respond matters. The energy you bring into a room matters. The choices you make in small, everyday moments matter more than you may have realized before. You begin to see that your life is not just a reflection of what you have been through, but a reflection of how you choose to move forward from it, and that realization brings a quiet kind of empowerment that cannot be taken from you.

There was a time in my life when reacting felt automatic, when emotions took over so quickly that there was no space for me to think, no space to choose, no space to do anything but respond in the way I always had. That is no longer where I am, and you can get there too. Something can shifted inside of you, even if it is still growing, even if it is still becoming stronger with time. The knowledge, discipline and awareness is there now, and with awareness comes choice. You are no longer operating blindly. You are learning how to meet life in a way that reflects who you sincerely want to be, not just what you have been through.

I can't promise you that your life will be perfect. Life will still bring moments that challenge you. There will still be people who say things that do not sit right with you, situations that test your patience, and days that feel heavier than others. The difference is no longer found in what happens around you, but in what happens within you. You have the tools now. You are not the same person who once carried everything without understanding it. You are not the same person who believed that anger was the only way to protect yourself. There is a new space inside of you now, one that allows you to pause, to breathe, and to choose differently. If you are being honest with yourself, you can feel it. You can feel that you are not as quick to react as you used to be. You can feel that there are moments where you catch yourself before things escalate. You can feel that there is something softer inside of you that was always there, something that never left, something that just needed to be uncovered. That is growth and you should be proud of yourself.

This is the new you. You are a great person, not the moments you regret. Not the reactions you wish you could take back. Not the labels that were placed on you or the ones you placed on yourself when you did not know any better. Those were experiences. Those were responses.

Those were chapters, but they were never your identity.

You are allowed to grow beyond who you used to be. You are allowed to wake up tomorrow and choose to show up differently than you did yesterday. You are allowed to release the version of yourself that was shaped by pain and step into the version of yourself that is guided by awareness, by intention, and by something deeper that has always existed within you.

No matter what you have done, no matter how you have reacted, no matter how long you carried that version of yourself, it does not disqualify you from becoming something better.

It simply means you are human, and as long as you have breath in your body, you can become whoever you choose to be Now!

About the Author

SaBrina Fisher Reece was once known throughout California as "The Braid Queen." For more than twenty-six years, she owned and operated the legendary Braids By SaBrina, a celebrated salon and school on Adams Boulevard in Los Angeles. It grew into the largest and most influential braiding establishment in the city, where artistry, empowerment, discipline, and community came together in powerful ways. Her success was entirely self-made, built through perseverance, resilience, and vision, often without consistent external support or validation.

As she stepped into the second half of her life, SaBrina felt a deeper calling unfolding within her. The story behind her success was not just one of entrepreneurship, but one of faith, healing, self-trust, and spiritual awakening. Early experiences of abandonment and profound personal loss led her inward, where she began the real work of emotional healing and inner mastery. What started as creative expression evolved into purposeful transformation.

Today, SaBrina writes self-help books rooted in emotional healing, personal growth, and spiritual awareness. Blending lived experience with motivational insight and metaphysical understanding, she explores themes of balance, resilience, self-mastery, and the unseen forces that shape human thought and behavior. Through her writing and motivational speaking, she guides readers toward deeper self-awareness, renewed confidence, and lives that feel intentional and aligned from the inside out.

She is the author of numerous self-help and transformational works, including *My Spiritual Smile, Kicking Depression In the Butt, Your Mind Is Magic, Perfectly Positive, Living Life on a Higher Frequency, Spiritual Balance, Angry World, Become Your Own Cheerleader,* God is Not a Man: Rediscovering the Divine Balance of Masculine and Feminine Within Us All, *Self Sabotage, How to Get Exactly What You Want From God, When I Say "I Am"*, and the popular Ebooks: *Imagine: Learn How to Use Your Imagination to Design the Life You Desire, You're Not Religious -You're Spiritual-I Get It: Bridging the Gap Between the Two, , Take A Breath With Bri: The Power of Intentional Breathing, Is This Why They Burned The Books?: Buried Wisdom From The Past.*

Her passion for sound and frequency has led her to explore the healing power of crystal sound bowls, tuning forks, and flow chimes, tools designed to help harmonize the body, mind, and spirit. Now residing in the enchanting landscapes of New Mexico, "The Land of Enchantment," she offers Sound Vibration Sessions that invite others to slow down, breathe deeply, and reconnect with their higher selves. While she embraces these modalities, she reminds her students and readers that there is no single path to peace. Every journey is sacred, and every sincere method of connecting with the Divine carries value.

Above all, SaBrina is a devoted mother of four, Justin, Joi, Jayden, and Journey, and a proud grandmother to Raiden Jesse and Rio Jordan. Watching them, and those she teaches, awaken to their divine potential remains her greatest joy.

Her message is simple and enduring: we are each born with divine energy, a God-given power to create, to heal, and to live fully. The goal is not perfection, but peace. The journey is not to escape life, but to embrace it, to use positive tools to take control of the mind and become the master of your fate.

You can connect with me on:

- https://in59secondspublishing.com
- https://www.facebook.com/BooksBySaBrinaFisherReece

Also by SaBrina Fisher Reece

SaBrina Fisher Reece was once known throughout California as *"The Braid Queen."*

For over twenty-six years, she owned and operated the legendary **Braids By SaBrina**, a celebrated salon and school on Adams Boulevard in Los Angeles. It became the largest and most influential braiding establishment in the city, a place where artistry, empowerment, and community beautifully intertwined.

As SaBrina stepped into the second half of her life, she felt a divine calling to share the deeper story behind her success, a journey of faith, transformation, and inner peace. What began as a career of creativity evolved into a life of purpose. She now inspires others through her writing and motivational speaking, guiding people toward healing and self-discovery.

How to Balance Good and Evil Understanding the Polarity of Human Nature and Choosing the Higher Path

What if "good" and "evil" are not distant forces fighting somewhere outside of you-but daily choices happening quietly within you?

In this powerful and deeply personal book, SaBrina Fisher Reece explores the truth about human nature: we are all born into a world of polarity. Light and shadow. Compassion and cruelty. Fear and love. The tension is not proof that you are broken—it is proof that you have been given free will.

This book does not label people as evil. It does not shame anger, frustration, or human imperfection. Instead, it teaches you how to recognize the internal tug-of-war we all experience and how to consciously choose the higher path without denying your humanity.

Through raw personal stories, leadership lessons, parenting moments, business experiences, and spiritual insight, SaBrina reveals how polarity shows up in everyday life-at work, in relationships, in traffic, in conflict, and even in your own thoughts. She demonstrates that self-regulation, compassion, emotional control, and imagination are powerful tools that help you move toward integrity instead of impulse.

You will learn:

How to understand the "dark side" without being ashamed of it

Why emotional control is a life-saving skill

How small daily choices shape your character

The difference between reacting and choosing

How compassion creates a better world without tolerating abuse

Why discipline is required to consistently choose your higher self

This book is for men, women, and young people who want to grow spiritually without judgment or religious condemnation. It is for those who understand that while horrific acts exist in the world, no one is born destined for darkness. We are given a choice every day.

You wake up at the center of the pole.

The direction you lean becomes the person you become.

If you are ready to understand yourself more deeply, lead with your heart, and consciously choose the higher side of who you are, this book will guide you there.

Sacred, Not Separate

How Religion and Spirituality Interact in Modern Life

What if the line between religion and spirituality was never meant to divide us?

In a world where people argue over doctrine, label one another, and separate themselves based on belief systems, *Sacred, Not Separate* offers a deeply personal and unifying perspective. This book is not about choosing sides. It is about bridging them.

Raised in the Christian Church of God in Christ by her grandmother, Bri Reece grew up rooted in faith, gospel music, prayer, and reverence for God. Later, through world travel, personal trauma, spiritual exploration, and profound healing experiences, she encountered meditation, sound healing, breath work, and ancient earth based practices that expanded her understanding of the divine.

Instead of abandoning religion for spirituality, or rejecting spirituality for religion, she discovered something powerful:

They are not enemies.

They are expressions.

Through raw storytelling and emotional honesty, Bri explores:

The illusion of division between church and spiritual practice

The power of sound in both gospel worship and sound healing

How trauma can make us vulnerable to spiritual ego

The importance of discernment in both religious institutions and spiritual centers

Breath as the universal bridge between body and spirit

Why meditation and prayer are more alike than we think

How belief shapes our lived experience

Why love is the only true spiritual barometer

This book courageously addresses spiritual manipulation, grief, healing, world travel, cultural perspective, and the personal responsibility we all carry in creating peace. It challenges the idea that God belongs to one structure, one language, or one group of people.

If your beliefs make you kinder, they are aligned.

If they make you cruel, something is off.

It is that simple.

Sacred, Not Separate is for the person who loves Jesus but also meditates.

For the one who wears a cross and a crystal.

For the family member tired of arguing at the dinner table.

For the seeker who refuses to be boxed in.

This is not a debate.

It is a bridge.

If you are ready to embrace unity without losing your foundation, to deepen your faith without shrinking your curiosity, and to live from a place of one God and one love, this book will meet you exactly where you are.

The sacred was never separate.

We just forgot.

God is not A Man

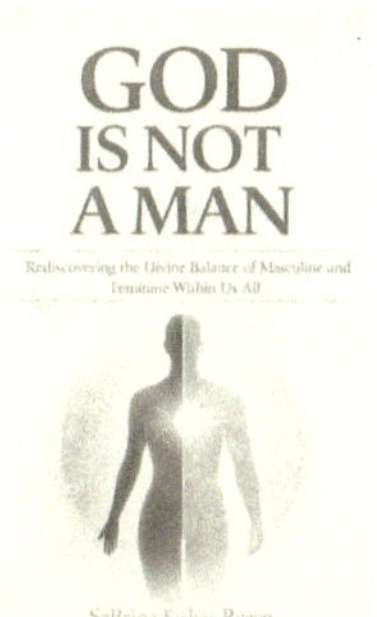

Is God exclusively male, or have we limited the image of the divine through tradition and culture?

In *God Is Not a Man: Rediscovering the Divine Balance of Masculine and Feminine Within Us All*, SaBrina Fisher Reece explores a powerful and often overlooked truth: divine source is not confined to gender. Drawing from scripture, ancient wisdom, global spiritual traditions, personal travel experiences, and modern psychological insight, this book challenges inherited assumptions while honoring faith.

Reece takes readers on a journey through Egypt, Greece, Indonesia, and Peru in search of a deeper understanding of God. Along the way, she examines universal law, the balance of masculine and feminine energy, and the spiritual maturity required to hold faith without limiting it. With clarity and conviction, she reveals how imbalance in our understanding of divine image has shaped theology, identity, and culture.

This book offers healing for women who have felt spiritually secondary and freedom for men who have felt pressured to suppress emotional depth. It speaks to the seeker who longs for truth without abandoning reverence. It affirms that strength and tenderness, authority and compassion, structure and intuition are not opposites but complementary expressions of one infinite source.

Rather than rejecting tradition, *God Is Not a Man* expands it. Rather than attacking faith, it deepens it. Readers will come away empowered, grounded, and more comfortable in their own wholeness, understanding that divine image is far greater than any single label.

For those ready to move beyond limitation and into balance, this book offers clarity, humility, and spiritual confidence.

MIND is ALL

In Mind Is All: Manipulating Ideas in a New Direction, SaBrina Fisher Reece explores the mechanics of thought-how ideas form, how they gain power, and how they quietly shape decisions, behavior, and belief. This book focuses less on positivity as a concept and more on mental leadership: learning how to consciously guide thought before it guides you.

Rather than motivating through inspiration alone, this book challenges readers to examine where their attention goes and why. It offers a framework for recognizing habitual thinking and deliberately steering it in a new, more constructive direction.

In this book, you'll learn how to:

Identify ideas that limit your growth
Redirect mental momentum instead of fighting it
Strengthen focus and internal discipline
Replace unconscious reactions with intentional thought
Use awareness to influence outcomes and decisions

Mind Is All is about reclaiming authority over your inner world. When you learn how ideas are formed and sustained, you gain the ability to reshape them-and in doing so, reshape your experience of life.

This book is for readers ready to think differently, not just feel better.

Pressure Down Plates Up
Delicious Meals for Lower Blood Pressure

High blood pressure does not mean giving up flavor.

It does not mean bland food, boring meals, or feeling restricted at the dinner table. It means learning how to cook smarter, season differently, and nourish your body in a way that supports your heart.

In *Pressure Down Plates,* you will discover delicious, satisfying meals designed to help lower blood pressure naturally-without sacrificing taste. This cookbook focuses on simple ingredients, practical swaps, and flavorful combinations that make heart-healthy eating feel enjoyable instead of overwhelming.

Inside you'll find:

Low-sodium meals packed with flavor

Smart seasoning alternatives that don't rely on excess salt

Simple recipes for busy weeknights

Wholesome ingredients that support heart health

Easy dishes the whole family will love

Whether you are newly diagnosed, managing long-term hypertension, or simply wanting to be proactive about your health, this book gives you meals you can actually look forward to eating.

Taking care of your heart should feel empowering-not limiting.

Lower the pressure. Lift your plates. Enjoy your food again.

How to Make More Money in 2026
Creating Residual Income from Your Home is a motivational, step-by-step mindset and money guide for everyday people who are ready to stop surviving and start building. This is not "get rich quick." This is "get focused, get aligned, and get paid for what you already know."

Inside, SaBrina Fisher Reece walks you through the real shift that changes everything: the new wealth mindset for 2026. Because before money shows up in your account, it has to show up in your thinking. You'll learn how to move from scarcity to strategy, how to turn your skills into real income streams, and how to build income that keeps working even when you are resting.

This book breaks down how residual income is created through digital products, smart systems, automation, branding, and consistent cash flow habits that don't require a fancy background or a perfect life. You'll learn how to monetize what you already know, package your value, and build from your home with the tools you already have.

What makes this book different is the voice behind it. SaBrina built her life through entrepreneurship, and she shares the truth from experience. After decades of running a successful salon and becoming an author, she launched In59Seconds Publishing Company from her computer at home, at her cute little pink desk, proving that reinvention is possible at any age and any stage. If she can learn it, you can learn it too.

If you're ready to make 2026 the year you stop watching other people win, and start building a legacy from your living room, this book is for you.

You don't need permission. You need a decision.

Small Business Basics

How to Start and Sustain a Small Business: is the book every new entrepreneur wishes they had on day one. In this powerful, real-world guide, SaBrina Fisher Reece - founder of Braids By SaBrina, A New Vision Dreadlock Studio, Just-In Time Barber Shop, In59Seconds Publishing Company, Inked 4 Life Tattoo Studio - shares the exact blueprint she used to build and sustain multiple successful businesses over 30 years.

This is not theory or fluff.

This is lived experience - straight from a woman who started with nothing but grit, faith, and a gift from God.

Inside these pages, SaBrina teaches you how to:

✔ Start your business with confidence

✔ Build structure, systems, and strong policies

✔ Attract clients with real marketing (not gimmicks)

✔ Lead with authority, heart, and integrity

✔ Set prices that reflect your worth

✔ Stay consistent, disciplined, and profitable

✔ Avoid the common mistakes that destroy small businesses

SaBrina has hired, trained, and mentored more than **1,700 employees**, survived betrayals, grown through heartbreak, and built an empire that became a household name in Los Angeles. Her lessons are raw, honest, spiritual, and rooted in the belief that **anyone can build a business - if they have the courage to start and the discipline to stay consistent.**

Whether you're launching your first idea, fixing a struggling business, or leveling up your brand, this book gives you the mindset, strategy, and motivation to succeed.

Your dream is possible.

Your vision is valid.

Your future is waiting.

Start today - Not tomorrow.

Stop Begging, Start Building

From Excuses to Execution in a World That Owes You Nothing

Somewhere along the way, asking became easier than building.

Cash App links at the top of videos. Fundraisers for rent. Public requests for everyday responsibilities. What once was reserved for emergencies has quietly become normal.

But here is the truth no one wants to say out loud.

Begging will never build the life you want.

In Stop Begging, Start Building, Bri Reece delivers a powerful wake up call wrapped in tough love and real life experience. After building a business from folding tables and door to door flyers into a thirty year success, reinventing herself multiple times, and refusing to rely on rescue, she challenges readers to reclaim their power, their discipline, and their responsibility.

This is not about shaming people for needing help. It is about breaking a mindset that keeps capable adults stuck in cycles of lack.

Inside this book, you will learn:

-Why public begging reinforces a poverty mindset

-How entitlement quietly erodes confidence

-Why prosperity begins in the mind before it reaches your bank account

-How to turn your existing skills into income

-Why quick money systems are designed to keep you behind .

-How faith and effort work together, not separately

This book speaks to anyone who feels stuck, frustrated, or dependent on circumstances outside their control. It challenges you to stop waiting, stop blaming, and start executing.

No one is coming to save you, and that is the best news you will ever hear. Because the power to build has been in you all along.

If you are ready to trade excuses for execution and dependency for discipline, this book will light the fire you have been waiting for.

Stop begging. Start building. Start living.

www.ingramcontent.com/pod-product-compliance
Lightning Source LLC
LaVergne TN
LVHW050938080826
845145LV00004B/1321